Without her love, I would be
as miserable as a Hairy Thing at a barber's /
would bravely fight back tears as I headed
for the football game / would spend more
time with my stamp collection.

And so I promise her my eternal, undying love /
to learn where the cups are kept /
to try to remember our anniversary.

Signed...

Date...

Other giftbooks in this series

My gorgeous guy
I love you madly
Go Girl!
My friend
Sorry
Little things mean a lot
Birthday Girl!
Birthday Boy!

Published in 2009 by Helen Exley Giftbooks in Great Britain.
Illustrations by Caroline Gardner © Caroline Gardner Publishing 2005
Illustrations by Roger Greenhough © Helen Exley 2009
All illustrations are based on the Caroline Gardner Elfin range
Text, selection and arrangement © Helen Exley 2009
The moral right of the author has been asserted.

12 11 10 9 8 7 6 5 4 3 2

ISBN: 978-1-84634-241-7

A copy of the CIP data is available from the British Library on request.
Words by Stuart and Linda Macfarlane
Edited by Helen Exley
Pictures by Caroline Gardner and Roger Greenhough
Printed in China
Helen Exley Giftbooks, 16 Chalk Hill, Watford, Herts WD19 4BG, UK
www.helenexleygiftbooks.com

Funny little people...

My lovable lady

By Stuart &
Linda Macfarlane

A HELEN EXLEY
GIFTBOOK

Imperfect you.

I love your little imperfections... every sing

ne of them!

Your jokes are always epics
with weak and woolly punch-lines
 but I would listen to them all day
 just to hear your voice.

The birthday presents
you give me are always
perfectly useless,
perfectly impractical
and perfectly wonderful.

Thanks for helping
to decorate our flat.
Doing it together was very special
– even though you hung
the wallpaper squiff
and covered the television in paint.

You show your love
in so many ways…
A big cup of tea.
Unexpected flowers.
Stolen kisses.
Unjustified compliments.
Just being you.

When you've had a bad hair day.
When tears have ruined
your mascara.
When a big red spot swells up
on your nose.
When you're wearing your
'comfort clothes'.
These are the times
when I love you most.

Six hours choosing an outfit.
One hour showering.
Two hours doing her hair.
One hour applying make up.
It's my lovely lady's
Big Night Out!

She goes to the big stores
and kits herself out
with expensive designer gear.
And especially all the hats.
Of course
she doesn't want to wear them –
she doesn't want to
ruin her hairstyle.

My special lady
doesn't 'shop till she drops'.
No, she stops
the moment her bags become
too heavy
for me to carry.

Trouble:

My very special woman
can get me out of any tricky situation –
well at least the ones
she gets me into.

When I wake up
my first thoughts are of her.
What will we do today?
Where will we go?
Will I go broke today?

Silence:

A period of time
      when my V.I.P.'s
        not talking to someone –
measured in microseconds.

When I say that I'm ready to go out
I mean that I'm ready to go.

When my little lady says this
she means that she'll be ready to go out,
as soon as she has had her bubble bath,
found her earring,
and had another cup of tea...

Lazy day:

Runny egg, cold tea, yip,

but who notices when it's

breakfast in bed again.

And the promise of a cuddle

and a good read in bed...

Loves me lots!

She has the patience of a saint,

the strength of an army

and all my

CD collection.

Love is... entrusting h

ith the remote control.

Just an ordinary day:

My gal and I can spend a day
    doing nothing
            and saying very little
– these can be
        the best times of all.

My lovely lady
is the glue
that holds my world together.
She would do anything,
dare anything
just to make me strong,
to be there for me.

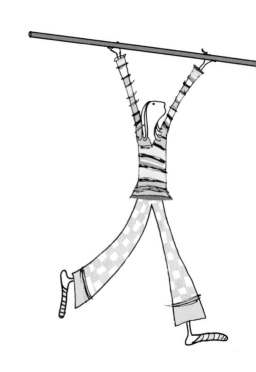

In today's politically correct society
it's no longer acceptable
to call my special helpmate a housewife
or even homemaker.
No. Nothing short
of Magnificent-Supreme-
Goddess-of-Charming-Loveliness
will do.

She doesn't smoke, drink or swear.
She has only
         one bad habit
                  – me!

When I'm covered in engine oil.
When I have a four day stubble.
When my hair is unkempt and greasy.
These are the times
she wraps me in her arms
and loves me most.

She thinks I'm perfect
– but then
why should I let her know
that she's wrong?

She does not try to cheer me
with witty words.
She merely holds my hand
and braves it through
the troubled times.

Always eager to please me,
        my chief chef took
a month long cookery class.
    Now she can burn 'Beans on Toast
Topped with
        Expensive Cheese'.

If she had to choose
between a shopping trip
without me
or an afternoon with me
she would choose to be with me...
but I know her thoughts
would be on the little black dress
that got away.

She's great at the big decisions
like which house or car to buy
but when it comes
to choosing shoes
to match an outfit
– boy, sometimes it takes days.

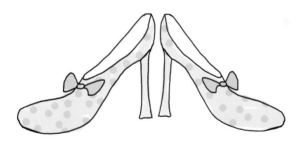

Silly moo

To a woman
      a map is something
that changes 'being lost'
            into 'being totally lost
and completely confused'.

When my sweetie's stressed...
she heads to the shopping mall
for some retail therapy.
When she's feeling calm...
she heads to the shopping mall
for some retail therapy.

My wonder woman
       is terrified of thunder
                     and lightning.
       But she deals with it
in a very mature way
              – she hides under the bed.

I never forget
my lovely lady's birthday
　　　　– her daily text
and Email messages
　　are a good reminder.

My domestic goddess
is always busy cleaning and washing
and ironing and mending.
Fortunately it hasn't occurred to her
that if she got rid of me
she could be reading books
and drinking cappuccino...

A crowded room,
anonymous faces, strangers.
A single word,
a smile,
a soul-mate.

She:

I see her smile
or hear her voice and know
that I am blessed.

She is my reason
for rising in the morning,
my reason for breathing,
my reason for living.

Sugar and spice and chocolate cake

hat's what my girl's made of.

Adoration: To love someone so much th

u see their blemishes as works of art.

I'm not strong.
She's not strong.
But together
we make the strongest force
in the known universe.

Love does not come
gift wrapped from
exclusive designer boutiques.
Love is found in ordinary places
by ordinary people living
ordinary lives.
Yet love is most special.
Beyond price.

Helen Exley runs her own publishing company
which sells giftbooks in more than seventy countries.
Helen's books cover the many events and emotions in life.
Caroline Gardner's delightfully quirky "elfin" cards
provided the perfect illustrations that Helen needed to go
ahead with her "Funny little people..." books. From there this
series of stylish and witty giftbooks quickly grew.

Caroline Gardner Publishing has been producing beautifully
designed stationery from offices overlooking the River Thames
in England since 1993 and has been developing the distinctive
"elfin" stationery range over the last nine years.
There are also many new illustrations created especially for
these books by artist Roger Greenhough.

Stuart and Linda Macfarlane live in Glasgow, Scotland.
They have produced several books with Helen Exley
including *My gorgeous guy*, *My friend*, *Birthday Boy!*,
Birthday Girl!, *Sorry* and the hugely successful
Utterly adorable cats.